UNDERSTANDING

YOUR 12-14 YEAR-OLDS

UNDERSTANDING

YOUR 12-14 YEAR-OLDS

Margot Waddell

Warwick Publishing

Toronto   Los Angeles

ISBN 1-894020-12-X

Published by:
Warwick Publishing Inc., 388 King Street East, Toronto, Ontario M5V 1K2
Warwick Publishing Inc., 1424 N. Highland Avenue, Los Angeles, CA 90027

Distributed by:
Firefly Books Ltd., 3680 Victoria Park Avenue, Willowdale, Ontario M2H 3K1

First published in Great Britain in 1993 by:
Rosendale Press Ltd.
Premier House
10 Greycoat Place
London SW1P 1SB

Design: Diane Farenick

Printed and bound in Canada

CONTENTS

TAVISTOCK CLINIC

The Tavistock Clinic, London, was founded in 1920, in order to meet the needs of people whose lives had been disrupted by the First World War. Today, it is still committed to understanding people's needs though, of course, times and people have changed. Now, as well as working with adults and adolescents, the Tavistock Clinic has a large department for children and families. This offers help to parents who are finding the challenging task of bringing up their children daunting and has, therefore, a wide experience of children of all ages. It is firmly committed to early intervention in the inevitable problems that arise as children grow up, and to the view that if difficulties are caught early enough, parents are the best people to help their children with them.

Professional Staff of the Clinic were, therefore, pleased to be able to contribute to this series of books to describe the ordinary development of children, to help in spotting the growing pains and to provide ways that parents might think about their children's growth.

INTRODUCTION

Caught between lost childhood and unrealized adulthood, the twelve to fourteen year-old often experiences the most conflict and the most bewildering and challenging years of all. They may be just as bewildering, as full of conflict and challenging to parents attempting to understand them as they are to the young adolescents themselves—torn between both wanting, and not wanting, to be understood.

This is a period of new kinds of friendship, of burgeoning sexuality, of changing interests and beginning awareness. It is a time of transition from a place in the family to a place in the outside world: a time of anxiety, apprehension and expectation, of the fear and thrill of the unknown. It is a time when, physically, growth is occurring more rapidly than at any other stage except in the womb, and when, alongside that, changes in mental and emotional growth are most insistent and most demanding.

Boundaries are being tested, assumptions questioned, losses endured. The twelve-year-old "child," newly out of elementary school, is struggling to relate the old world to the new, undergoing an intimidating and intoxicating rite of passage, clinging to the familiar, fascinated by the untried. By fourteen, the "young person" may seem to have abandoned childish things and to be precariously launched into a personal and social world of immense complexity, but as yet with no clear goals or direction. The central preoccupation is one of identity— "who am I?"

The mother of a twelve-year-old boy and fourteen-year-old girl was heard to say to a friend with children of similar age, "I must get back to the kids. They seem to want me to be there even more now than when they were little. There's so much to say." "Good heavens," was the reply, "you don't mean your children still talk to you. I haven't the faintest idea what Jane and Ian are up to or what they're thinking about. I find myself just hoping for the best."

Most parents will recognize that the twelve to fourteen year-old, each in their own particular way, is going through dramatic changes and that the task of adapting to these changes is a hard one, for child and parent alike. Perhaps harder to recognize is that change is involved for themselves as well. Many parents will have been developing with their child all along. At this age, however, it becomes evident that the understanding that is so crucial to the child's sense of security and self-esteem is based more firmly than ever in the parents' continuing ability to question what they thought they knew, to bear not knowing, to examine themselves, to dare to change as well. Being the parent of a fourteen year-old often feels very different from being one of a twelve year-old—sometimes lonelier, sometimes richer. You may discover a different kind of friendship or you may feel tested to the limit—"I love you but I don't always like you," is a not unfamiliar cry!

How can all this be thought about, be understood? The thinking and the understanding may be experienced as more difficult and more painful than ever before. This book explores the social and emotional tasks of twelve to fourteen year-olds. It considers responses to the physical changes of puberty, to anxieties about sexuality, to problems of identity. It reflects on different kinds of friendship—on the relationship between the changing demands of school and of family life. It looks at the ordinary expressions of desire, doubt and enthusiasm characteristic of the age group, and at the ways in which things may go wrong, the pitfalls and worries both for children and parents—for example, drug abuse, eating problems, difficult behavior. It discusses the difficulty of maintaining a balance between the recognition and encouragement of greater freedom and the need for protection from the frightening possibilities that are suddenly opening up. Understanding what is likely to be going on for young people of this age may suggest ways in which parents may better enjoy, help and support them.

CHAPTER ONE

OTHER BODIES — OTHER SELVES

Fourteen year-olds tend to think about being twelve as belonging to the distant past, almost to a different person. These are typical reflections: "At twelve I expected to be looked after twenty-four hours a day." " I would do exactly what I wanted. " "I was treated like a child then, now I'm treated like a grown-up." "Now I'm into boys." "I was interested in being at home and in childish things, playing games like 'Hide and Seek.' Now I'm interested in competitive sports and going out with friends, just anywhere." "I used to be good but now I do things to upset people—being bad-tempered, unreasonable, selfish, teasing and calling people unpleasant names." "I'm more interested in my friends now than in my family." "I'm much more independent and calm about things now." "I didn't have many worries about boys. I do now and it takes over my work." "I was looked after then. Now I feel on my own." "When I was twelve, to attract a girl maybe I would act tough and be very physical. Now I would talk to them and listen to what they have to say." "I don't pine for my mom anymore." What is it that has really happened between being the dependent child, whose emotional and creature needs were taken care of "twenty-four hours a day," and being the young adolescent who is busy putting away "childish things" and who doesn't "pine for mom anymore"?

While most parents of twelve year-olds will have no difficulty acknowledging, often wistfully, that their child seems to be quite different from even a few months ago, they will find it much easier to describe *what* is happening than to have much sense of *why*. "She's suddenly started wearing baggy sweaters/body suits/dying her hair/wanting a nose ring." "He spends all his time in his room/ in front of a mirror/on the phone/reading magazines." "She's always starting fights about trivial things." "He won't wear the expensive jacket I bought only a few weeks ago," etc. The "children" may have as little idea as you about what is really going on. They find themselves feeling angrier, moodier, more anxious, more lonely, not "themselves." Their responses to this strange state of affairs and the form these responses take in the family, at school, in the outside world, will be talked about in later chapters. But it is important first to establish what really is happening at a basic, physical level, and then to look at the various means that are adopted to adjust to that process.

Puberty: bodily changes

A child may well ask, "What's happening to me?" for biological changes are occurring at this time over which he or she has no control—the physiological, anatomical, hormonal changes which are called "puberty." Puberty occurs in different bodies at different times and in different ways. It usually happens earlier for girls than for boys. Some nine-year-old girls are already menstruating, some do not begin until fifteen or sixteen. But for both boys and girls, the most usual time for puberty is between twelve and fourteen. Each is becoming sexually, though not necessarily emotionally, an adult. The girls begin to have periods, to develop breasts and pubic hair; the shape and contours of their bodies are rapidly changing, often with a sudden increase in weight. They are sweating, smelling and often suffering unfamiliar aches and cramps. The boys experience their first ejaculations (usually initially in wet dreams). They often have a sudden increase in growth, they fill out, develop bodily hair, possibly acne, their voices change. They too sweat and smell. They become awkward and clumsy in their unfamiliar bodies.

These are the external characteristics. The processes of adjustment to those characteristics, emotionally and behaviorally, are what we call "adolescence." The responses to these external changes are seldom straightforward and they may be greeted with a wide variety of feelings—from denying it's happening at all, to dread, to apprehension, to relief, to delight. Usually the feelings are mixed: pride and disgust, excitement and worry and, above all, self-consciousness.

Typical anxieties

Fathers often know little of these reactions. Mothers may know more about their daughters than their sons, but even then the anxious question at bedtime about whether it's "normal to have one nipple bigger than the other," or "I've got a hard lump on one side and not the other—do you think it's cancer?" tends to represent the very tip of an iceberg of puzzles, confusions, anxieties, comparisons and mysteries. Acquaintance with the so-called facts of life by this age should not be confused with a belief that the young person in question really understands what is going on. We may feel that teachers, or preferably we ourselves, have described to these young interrogators all that is necessary about sexual development, intercourse and reproduction. But such factual explanations tend to be a very different matter from the actual experience of the bodily changes and sexual feelings that are occurring in them as individuals. They are different too from the enormous variety of questions which arise in relation to the now most important and interesting person in the world, namely themselves.

"Tracy says you can't go swimming if you have a period." "If you masturbate does it mean you can't have a baby?" "Susan says if the blood's brown to start with it means you'll be infertile." These are some girls' remarks with which many mothers will be very familiar. The boys tend to be less open about things, no less with fathers than with mothers. Brothers and sisters are suddenly chased out of the bathroom and the door is locked. Requests are made for healthier food. Unexpected questions are posed: "Is cereal good for you?" "Do chips give you zits?" The reason for no longer wanting to go swimming eventually turns out not to be the chlorine, as stated, but the spotty back. "Mom, none of the other boys are circumcised," or "They've all got pubic hair except me," may be the rare and only indications of agonies in the showers, or the reason for suddenly not wanting to go to camp. "I'm not as tall as the others" will suddenly pop miserably out of what had seemed to be problems with math homework. Some boys will discuss with a parent why it is that an erect penis seems to shrink when in repose, but most will attempt, uncertainly, to glean such crucial information from other sources—films, books, gossip among friends of their own age, older boys.

Parents' responses

The sorts of comment just quoted represent an enormous range of conscious worries which parents may hear something of, and have to be ready to cope with and listen to as they arise. Yet it is usually important to be neither too probing nor too curious if the anxieties are not volunteered. A respectful, although not uninterested, distance is usually required, particularly with the boys, one which nonetheless conveys concern and a readiness to talk, should the occasion arise.

Children may no longer feel that parents are the appropriate figures to turn to for answers to these new questions about the onset of puberty. The reasons are often quite disparaging: "they'd be too embarrassed," "they wouldn't know anyway." Or they may indicate vulnerability: "they might laugh at me." But the true sources of this distancing of parents from the young person's intimate life are complex ones, belonging to another level of feeling which underlies the more conscious ones just discussed. The hormonal and chemical changes which bring about physical growth and development at this time also reactivate passionate feelings and impulses, basically of love and hate, which were typical of the infant and very young child's relation to his or her parents. The commonly heard despairing cry of the thirteen year-old's parents, "Oh stop being so infantile," is perhaps more accurate than is often realized.

The young adolescent's changes revive a confusion of early longings towards, and aversions from, each parent, the intensity of which may be as baffling to the young person in question as it is disturbing to you. This intensity is related to the fact that there are now particular dangers attached to these passions which make them especially hard to manage. For the sexually mature body of the young teenager has become technically able to realize the longings and carry out the aversions. The social necessity to begin separating from parent and family and to find a place in the social world is thus also fueled by the much more primitive and unconscious necessity to let go of the parent, or parents, as figures to whom their primary loving and hating feelings are directed and eventually to find substitutes for them elsewhere.

CHAPTER TWO

SEXUALITY

The physical changes of puberty bring the issue of sexuality center stage. Although, in a sense, they have been sexual beings from the moment of their birth, the twelve to fourteen year-old feels his or her sexuality to be like an entirely new, often dreadful, often exciting, experience. For it is sexual curiosity, sexual urges and sexual anxieties which most powerfully affect and fuel their relationships to themselves, their parents, friends and friendship groupings as never before. And it is often parents' complicated feelings about their own sexuality, both past and present, that make it hard to adopt a helpful attitude towards their young adolescent.

There are some similarities in the boy's and the girl's sexual experience at this stage, but there are also some very important differences. Both, for example, are struggling to sort out their masculine and feminine sides. The struggle will certainly have been present in younger years, but with the arrival of puberty it becomes more pressing to resolve because of the need to establish sexual identity in relation to thinking about actual sexual partners. Both boys and girls are also engaged with letting go not just the relationship with their parents as central and special, but at a more primitive level they are again having to deal with the earliest relationship to their mother. Feelings of blissful at-oneness and of savage rivalry are stirred up again—sometimes expressed to the mother herself and to her relationship with her husband or partner, sometimes to other figures, who in some way stand for the parental couple in the young person's fantasy.

Very early, often largely unconscious, fears and fantasies are reactivated at this time. They tend to find expression in dreams rather than in conscious thought, or in films such as *Jaws* or *Jurassic Park* which, in explicitly playing on such themes, are often of particular fascination to this age group.

The central anxiety for the boy is often that of being shut up inside a bad place, being stuck, trapped, losing his penis and/or his mind. The girl may have fears of invasion or occupation by something terrifying which will get inside and wreak havoc, in particular destroying the possibility of her having babies. In that each sex also, to some extent, identifies with the other, versions of these fantasies may be shared. Such images, thoughts and fantasies are a long way from actual tender, loving and caring relationships and one of the central conflicts of this age group tends to be that of how to reconcile these two very different sorts of impulse and feeling.

Masturbation

One source of relief from the tensions aroused may be through masturbation—touching and finding sexual pleasure in parts of their own bodies, particularly their genitals. The guilt that this often stirs up may not be so much about the masturbation itself as about the day dreams and fantasies that accompany it. For sexual thoughts at this age often have aggressive, lurid or perverse aspects to them which the young person finds unfamiliar and disturbing. A kind of mental experimentation goes on, fueled by the recent hormonal changes, which may become a source of unspoken conflict, in that the experience is both alarming and gratifying.

Masturbation usually disturbs parents too—who perhaps forget, or don't wish to remember, how they felt themselves at that age. The time when masturbation was prohibited, always pointless, has, on the whole, passed and there is now a more general recognition that beginning to masturbate is a very normal aspect of adolescence. The moment to be concerned may arise when the parent feels that masturbation, and the fantasies that go with it, is a substitute for making any real contact with others—contact based in feelings of affection or love as well as lust and desire. When a young adolescent indulges in frequent masturbation but with no sign of any actual relationship then some encouragement towards taking risks, or getting to know others as real people rather than as fantasized figures may be required. Really only the parents can know, almost by the "feel" of things, at what point to start worrying. Just as only a parent can know whether their child's interest in certain books, films and videos is one that they can take in their stride, or whether that interest is stirring up feelings which are hard for them to manage. It may be, for example, that sexual feelings have become attached to experiences of, or fears about, abandonment, conflict, rejection, guilt, recklessness, cruelty. This may be an expression of a difficulty of engaging with painful emotional areas which need to be recognized rather than avoided.

Unfortunately parents are seldom in a position to know what exactly these young people are exposing themselves to, or being exposed to by friends and older adolescents. Perhaps, however, it should be borne in mind that, despite misgivings, showing an interest in what might seem excessively explicit or even perverse areas of sexuality may have positive aspects too, to be understood rather than condemned. For young adolescents, like everyone else, have perverse thoughts and fantasies. It can be a relief to them to discover that such fantasies are commonly shared and expressed "out there." It may also be reassuring to have an opportunity to "rehearse" their fantasies about, for example, love-making by watching it on screen, or reading about it, before they come anywhere near actually doing anything about it themselves.

Over-protectiveness and denial on a parent's part may make it harder for a young person to experiment in fantasy, and to some extent in fact, with these exciting, frightening and often contradictory feelings. To take no responsibility at all, however, may be to allow them an excess of over-stimulating or arousing experiences—especially those involving violence or degradation—which can stir up considerable guilt. It is a rare adolescent who is able to talk to their parents about such things in detail. Fathers can sometimes try to share the smutty humor, or talk in a "macho" way with their sons about girls or sexy movies. But this can often feel intrusive and embarrassing. Mothers may get a bit further in discussing the emotional aspects of sexual experiences. But for the most part this is an area which, it should be assumed, is little shared though very preoccupying, significantly contributing to mood swings, bouts of unexpected anger, elation or withdrawal. It is hard for parents to be attentive while being neither probing nor prohibiting, but just available without standing in judgment.

Technically knowing the facts of life in no sense lessens the intense curiosity about all aspects of sexuality, especially the adult world. Both boys and girls will be very interested in adult sexuality, their investigations and fantasies usually being directed not so much towards their own parents as elsewhere. Indeed, the idea of parents having an ongoing sexual relationship together is seldom a welcome one. In conversation with her thirteen-year-old group of girlfriends, Laura stated that she was convinced that her parents hadn't "done it" since she was herself conceived. "Nor have mine," agreed some of the others. "But what about your little sister?" Sally asked. "Well maybe once," Laura replied. Laura was absolutely shattered and furious a few weeks later when her parents told her that they had decided to have a "last" baby. Apart from the understandable jealousy towards a younger rival, Laura was uncomfortably confronted with the fact of adult sexuality, not in general—which was a daily preoccupation for her and her friends—but in the particular case of her own parents.

What is often underestimated at this age is the loss that goes with the necessary displacing of parents from their central position in the child's inner world. Some degree of self-esteem was linked to the high regard in which they held their parents. With that now diminished there is often a dramatic drop in the sense of self worth—the feeling of emptiness or void so many adolescents describe. With one set of ties being loosened, and another not yet made, there is a period of transition in which self-preoccupation often predominates. Whether it is putting the self down or building it up, the adolescent "self" tends to be the greatest source of interest around.

Making new relationships

It is at this point that the differences between the two sexes have to be emphasized. First, the girl's sexual partner is very likely to be from the opposite sex to her mother, the boy's from the same sex. Secondly, in terms of his anatomy and his physical experiences, the boy will be much clearer about sexual desire—how it feels and how it is expressed—than the girl at this age. And thirdly, there are important cultural factors which have a major impact on each, in terms of what is expected of a girl and of femininity, and what of a boy and masculinity.

For the girl, as the tie to the mother loosens, the need is very strong for intense friendship with other girls. There is a tendency in fantasy to idealize, and often sexualize, older girls or young women who can replace what is being let go. There is a tendency too to be drawn to more powerful or more attractive girls whose dominant characters lend status to their views and activities.

But it should be remembered that the mother was not only the source of love but also of rage and frustration—feelings which now often get expressed about, and towards, girl friends. If the relationship with her mother has been good, a girl can more easily feel, particularly when her periods begin, that she can let go of her little-girl dependency on her mother and be like her in a more grown-up feminine way. Many mothers, however, are upset to experience what they feel to be their daughter's unexpected negativism at this stage. This very often occurs when the relationship in the past has not been easy and the young adolescent now finds herself both seeking, and fighting, a much earlier child-like relationship. She wants, in other words, to hold onto something from the past she feels she still needs—perhaps from a sense that she had never got enough. She may then feel angry and resentful about that holding on-to and needy feeling, and pull away again with unpredictable suddenness.

Whichever way it is, the complexity of this early relationship with the mother does contribute to a greater tendency for girls to get emotionally intensely entangled with other girls—more so than does a boy with his peer group. This perhaps links to the issue of just how cruel girls of this age can be to one another, how preoccupied they are with the daily dramas of treachery and betrayal. Much is required of such friends: loyalty, often exclusivity; partnership in secrets, possibly with a sexual content which heightens the excitement and the erotic flavor; sharing of fantasies—usually about boys or imagined adult sexual relationships. All this is reassuring. It makes them feel normal. They find in each other qualities which either confirm what they are like themselves or express what they would like to be like. The relationships the girl has with other girls, with teachers, female film stars and so on have elements of the original bond with mother but they exist at a safer distance.

On the whole, then, the inner world of the young girl is peopled by other females. It is an intensely sexual time: boys are exciting, fascinating, sometimes to be gone out with or snubbed, but primarily to be talked about, thought about and fantasized about. There are endless whispered conversations about who's "doing it," about what "it" might feel like, what sexual desire really is. Describing herself at fourteen,

Clare (now eighteen) expressed the feeling very clearly: "I felt totally miserable, either furious or self-hating all the time. Writing a diary was a bit of a help but what finally made the difference was finding Emily. We just did everything together. We told each other our secrets, our fantasies, our worst fears, things that we'd never tell anybody else. We went everywhere together; we slept in the same bed together. I'm sure I was kind of in love with her, but it wasn't sexual. She made all the difference to my world. Sometimes I even thought for a moment that I might be really beautiful like her, it was just that I didn't look it. We were part of a group of friends which were important too, but the really close relationship was always with our best friends—for me, Emily."

Clare's experience was not primarily sexual. But of course, it often is sexual in secret and exciting ways. There may be an intense wish to touch breasts as they compare growth and size for example. They may dream about other girls—experience first being "in love" in relation to girls, become fascinated with finding out about lesbian relationships.

For boys sex tends to be less mysterious. Having had erections from a young age they are in no doubt at all what sexual desire is, nor where it is located. Their groups are also close and similar to the girls,"in the sense that they tend to be made up of boys like themselves. Again similarities are reassuring when being different is so terrifying. On another level the loss of a sense of identity, which goes with letting go the world of childhood and the strong bond with his mother, is a bit reduced when surrounded by others who are somehow in his own image. With a boy this loss is also partly made up of the feminine side of his personality which he now feels he has to let drop along with his mother if he is to be confidently a man. The result is often a kind of exaggeration of "manly" qualities, especially clear in groups and often modeled on quite crude notions of manhood—probably very different from their actual fathers. A swaggering, "macho" character may make its appearance, with an unnaturally gruff voice, repertoire of swear-words and unfamiliar gait.

Homosexuality

The exaggerated manliness, on the other hand, is often also an expression of the anxiety, so typical of this age, about being homosexual. Most boys, and many girls, will, in the course of sorting out their confused desires and urges, have homosexual feelings and not uncommonly experiment with homosexual activities. This is often an important part of establishing "who's me." Although in relation to prevailing cultural norms, it may cause fear, guilt and distress, it should certainly be regarded as part of the ordinary process of growing up. The degree to which homosexuality is felt to be upsetting is importantly related to family and cultural attitudes, but the anxiety in the adolescents about something as basic as what gender they feel they are should not be underestimated.

A rather clear, albeit extreme, example of this is fourteen-year-old John, who had been very close to his dad until his parents marriage broke up when he was about twelve. As the oldest in the family, he had become very supportive of his mother who had four other younger children to look after. Soon after John's fourteenth birthday his teacher became worried about his missing so much school. She discovered from his mother that he had become uncharacteristically rude, rejecting and angry towards her and totally preoccupied with anxiety about being homosexual. It emerged that he had also become very worried about whether or not he had actually turned off the appliances in the house—especially faucets—and whether he had shut the door securely.

In the course of some sessions with the school counselor, John came to realize that although he hated the idea of being homosexual it was less frightening than experiencing physical desire towards his mother. He had first become aware of this desire in a surge of jealous rage when he saw a waiter flirtatiously touch his mother's bottom soon after his father had left home. His anger with his mother was a painful attempt to distance her from his passionate feelings, and to make her undesirable in his mind by demeaning her. Possibly his worry about turning things off was an expression of his fear of not being in control of his feelings generally, and, perhaps more specifically, his ejaculations.

Having understood some of this, John was able to direct his feelings towards a more appropriate person—a girl of his own age to whom he became attracted soon after his counseling sessions ended. The other worries became much more manageable. In this case John's dad was not physically there to assert paternal rights which might have inhibited his son's incestuous anxieties. Nor was he able to offer any emotional support to John because of the fury and disillusionment with his father for, as John saw it, abandoning the family home. John felt his dad was a failure and an object of contempt. His criticisms, only to some extent justifiable, were fueled by primitive feelings of anger, fear and hatred. His parents' marital difficulties had made the ordinary problems of sorting out his respective relationship to them a lot harder for, like everyone else, he had in his infancy painfully to acknowledge his father's supremacy and to take his place in relation not to his mother alone, which was what he desired, but to his parents as a couple. Having his mother again to himself had stirred up early guilts and anxieties which he found confusing and unmanageable.

Jack vividly remembered his discovery of prejudice over homosexuality in his own age group and how he was supported in sorting out his feelings by an understanding mother. He described the social difficulties he ran into when he started "making friends" at fourteen, instead of just "being close to the guys" on the school football team, which had nothing to do with intimacy. "At fourteen I started 'making friends' with girls instead of just 'going out with them.' I also made friends with an effeminate boy whom everyone thought was homosexual. But he was much more interesting than everyone else. Guys are often cruel at that age about difference. They stopped talking to me because I was a homosexual's friend. It would have been much easier for me not to be friends with this guy and I got very upset about it. Luckily, my mom was great. She said, 'You must keep him as your friend despite what others say.' My mom was a big influence on me. I suppose she was sort of overseeing things, but never overlooking them."

Old emotions, new feelings

The physical changes of puberty, then, arouse feelings which are powerful, new and therefore mysterious and alarming—alarming because they belong to areas of the unconscious, rooted in very early experience, and therefore not available to be thought about in the ordinary way. This may go some way to explaining the sense, so common at this age, of guilt and shame about something which remains somehow nameless. The twelve to fourteen year-old does not know what he or she is so ashamed about, or guilty of. There is no specific answer because that answer is likely to lie in these unknown areas of desire and rage in which often the conscious thought or masturbatory fantasy is somehow felt to be the same as actually having done something.

The small child's anxiety that whatever has gone wrong is basically their fault is often revived and intensified by these sexual and aggressive impulses. Looking back on these years, one nineteen year-old, Joanna, put it very well: "It was all very frightening. I thought 'I'm going crazy,' and 'it's all my fault.' 'No,' I thought, 'it's not my fault, it's my dad's fault' . . . whichever way it is, it's terrible.' I felt completely misunderstood all the time—either furious or self-hating, scared of what was going to happen. Would it be like this for the rest of my life? I denied what was happening to my body and at the same time agonized about whether there was something wrong in finding people sexy." Joanna had concerned and loving parents who would have thought of themselves as understanding and emotionally in touch. But they were also beginning to experience something that will be familiar to many parents: that the models they feel they can offer no longer seem relevant to their children.

What is often being sought in the various types of grouping at this age is some alternative source of identification from the stereotypes their parents are usually taken to represent. For instance, the girls may be struggling to find a positive identification which is neither only maternal nor merely sexy. For boys common male stereotypes may seem powerful and erotic, but also at odds with their own more tender and caring feelings. Whether boys or girls, one may be fairly certain that, in the area of sexuality in particular, between twelve and fourteen they are experiencing intense pressures coming from outside and inside simultaneously. One may be fairly sure, too, that the excitements and guilt will seldom be worked out with the parents directly. Bearing the exclusion may often be hard for parents. Often the best that can be done is for parents to be sensitive to what may be going on and respectful of their sons' or daughters' privacy.

CHAPTER THREE

SCHOOL LIFE

The elementary/secondary divide

Most children between the ages of twelve and fourteen find themselves much more drawn to their friends than to their family. They are making the transition at some point during these years from a known and familiar way of life to a new and strange one—from primary to elementary to junior and senior high school. In general parents find that they have much less to do with school life on a day-to-day basis than before—especially if they were used to meeting children in the playground, going into school and talking with teachers. Now they feel almost left out: they don't have a "feel" for the school or for the nature of their children's daily experiences .

For the parents, teachers often have names but no faces: the new rules, visible and invisible, are confusing; parents are no longer familiar with particular and likely sources of anxiety in their child. They may be aware that their twelve year-old is under strain but do not know its source nor how to help. More important, they are often no longer in a position where they can be of significant help. The elementary to secondary divide is much bigger than many anticipate. The change of school is often eagerly looked forward to. Many children have had enough of their old school by the time they reach the top, but for a large number the shock of entering "big school," and the different way of life it involves, takes a long time to adjust to—often the whole of the first year.

It is hard for parents to take in just what an impact this has. The comments at the beginning of Chapter 1 about wanting, at twelve, "to be looked after twenty-four hours a day" have to be considered in relation to how little looking-after they feel they now receive at school. Some find it very difficult to adjust, for example, to getting to school and back on their own; having a different teacher for each subject; occupying different classrooms, to and from which they have to carry all their belongings; dealing with expectations that they will take responsibility for communications within school and between home and school, and with assumptions that they will organize their homework properly.

Making friends

Above and beyond all these in importance, however, is likely to be the enormous social stress of making friends, of dealing with the pain and pleasure of being excluded or included, left out or popular. Having never particularly noticed or cared about differences of race, class or gender before, these factors suddenly begin to divide up the school community into factions, hierarchies, pecking orders. In secondary schools, for example, racial groupings and the particular styles that attach to them, in terms of fashion, language, music, interests and attitudes become much more obvious. Differences in family income also become more noticeable—enabling some to "do the clubs" and leaving others, of necessity, hanging out in parks or on street corners. With such differences bullying, petty crime and theft often begin, organized around particular groups or rather around particular gangs.

In short, twelve year-olds feel thrown in at the deep end to discover who they are in relation to what other children seem to feel about them. Few children have spent their early school years with no experience of bullying, but entry into secondary school, partly because it is so stressful for everyone, tends to sharpen children's responses to feelings of uncertainty and difference. Looking back from the comparative safety of nineteen, Jane described those early days: "I hated it really. It was such a burden looking confident when I didn't feel like that inside at all. Everyone was watching everyone *all* the time. I was aware of what I looked like practically every minute of the day. I always felt a complete outsider—not middle-class enough for one group, not working-class enough for the other, the wrong sex, the wrong race. It all felt terrible. Most of all, I suppose, I discovered just how cruel girls can be to other girls—nasty, in subtle, undermining sorts of ways that left me feeling miserable with no one to talk to about it."

Parents' attitude to school

All this is not to say that some children don't take to junior high or secondary school like ducks to water. But it is perhaps more usual, in the first year, for children to suffer in ways which their parents may have only a general sense of but with little idea of the detailed experiences. Sometimes they discover this indirectly, when, for example, their child mysteriously develops a series of tummy aches or headaches which seem to prevent them from going to school. It is hard for a parent to recognize that something may lie behind these "illnesses," and to have to face not being able to "make it better," as they might have done in the past. Their son or daughter now has to manage largely on their own. Yet struggling mainly without their parents' help—if not without their support—though painful, may for the young adolescent be an important way of finding their place in the world and sorting out who they are.

Despite feeling that their interest in school activities is no longer welcome, parents' attitudes to school life and teachers in fact remains very significant. Underneath the superficial casualness, the fourteen year-old usually *does* want parents to remember the name of the English teacher they have had for two years; to know roughly what is meant by the current slang, to recognize the sources of provocation and difficulty in their particular school—no toilet paper; water turned off for most of the day. Most of all they need an interest to be taken in their achievements rather than in their failings. Sam, whose father didn't live in the family anymore, was always extremely anxious about his dad's good opinion of him. With anticipated pleasure, he took his excellent grade eight report card over to show his father. "That's good, but why did you only get a C in French?" Sam was desperate. His father was never shown a report card again.

It is usually helpful for a child to feel that parents are basically sympathetic to the school despite its inevitable deficiencies, and also, generally, on the side of the teachers. They have to keep the difficult balance between neither totally handing over responsibility for their child to the school nor, in turn, undermining the school's authority. This may at times be hard, especially in the light of the hair-raising stories about teachers' behavior and attitudes that can be recounted by their youngster with considerable relish. Simply siding with either party is seldom a good solution. On the one hand if an authoritarian school regime is not questioned, it may seem to reinforce intolerant attitudes at home, leaving the child with nowhere to turn. Indeed this may lead to a child reproducing that same intolerance in his or her own group of friends. On the other hand it may not be the best way forward for parents always straightforwardly to accept the child's point of view despite the total conviction with which it may be being stated. At this age everything is likely to be dramatized—seen in extremes of good and bad and, above all, highly changeable.

In spite of this it is also very important for a child of this age to feel that their views, say, of a teacher's unjust behavior, are being taken seriously, neither written off as "that's life" nor made into a federal offense. Twelve to fourteen year-olds often have an admirably fierce, though perhaps crude, sense of justice and some encouragement to see things tolerantly, or at least imaginatively, from different angles is always helpful. If glaring injustices continue to be complained about over a period of time, then action may be required. There is always a fine line between parental interference and the abdication of concern and responsibility. Nonetheless, it is hard to get it right. Do you reprimand a child who is persecuting your daughter? Do you call up her parents? Do you tell your daughter to stick it out? Or do you go to the school to complain? Resistant though they may seem to be, most children are reassured to feel parents and school are co-operating. They also need to feel their parents, whether still together or not, are basically in agreement over their schooling along with their general welfare.

Thirteen-year-old Danny vividly described his pride and horror when his mom stormed into the principal's office to complain about his being victimized. Despite embarrassment, there may be great relief when a firm line is taken. It requires careful judgment to decide when a child's complaint about being teased or badly treated at school is something a child should be encouraged to stand up to, and when it is a matter of being singled out and picked on to an unacceptable and cruel degree. Such a distinction usually requires sensitivity, over a period of time, to that particular child's moods and behavior—whether there is a sense of depression, a reluctance to go to school, deterioration in work and so on. This, combined with discussion with the home room teacher or staff concerned may help to sort out how serious the problem is and whether one child has become the butt of particularly unkind attention. Despite resistance there is often considerable relief when a parent intervenes in such matters, particularly if the school's response is swift and appropriate.

Jenny's parents noticed that for some weeks she had been sleeping badly, was prone to tears and unusually reluctant to go to school. To their gentle inquiries, she maintained for some time that nothing was wrong and would they please leave her alone. But late one night, she described to her mother her feeling upset about boys in her class picking on her and calling her names of a particularly crude, racist kind. Jenny swore her mother to secrecy—she would die rather than have it known that she was troubled by this or had told tales.

The distress continued, however, and her mother, having discussed it with a couple of other parents, decided to mention her concern to the home room teacher. The teacher's response was to discuss the matter with the whole class, not in relation to Jenny's individual experience but as an issue of great concern to the school. Any more signs of such behavior would, in the future, be very firmly dealt with. Jenny was immensely relieved that her parents and the school had co-operated without betraying her confidence with the result that she herself had to take neither the responsibility nor the blame.

It may, on the other hand, be the teacher who alerts the parents to problems a child is having with others in, or outside, the classroom. Teachers are in a special position to observe relations among these young teenagers and have immediate access to the many aspects of their lives which are now becoming less available to parents.

Indeed teachers during these years may often have a very central role in a child's life. The capacity on their part to be receptive to the complex forms a child's communications may take, to understand and respond to those communications for what they really are, rather than what they may appear to be on the surface, can have an enormous impact on the individual child's school experience. The teacher occupies a very important position as someone who is outside the immediate family, but has extensive experience of twelve to fourteen year-olds' feelings, behavior and social relations, as well as their cognitive skills and intellectual development.

Difficulty in any of these areas may be the first signal to a sufficiently sensitive teacher of some sort of anxiety, possibly needing to be addressed with the individual child and, if appropriate, with the family as well. Such a teacher may also be aware of the stresses and conflicts which often underlie behavior problems generally. The feeling of being understood rather than punished or disciplined may then support stronger and more hopeful development rather than fearfulness and despondency.

At fourteen, Nick was caught smoking cannabis with a group of friends. Not only was this in the school grounds but in a particular spot which was in full view of the staffroom. He was very severely reprimanded, his parents were sent for and he was suspended from school for a week. His father realized this uncharacteristically delinquent behavior could be linked to the fact that Nick had been mugged earlier in the week by some older boys. His watch and sneakers had been taken and he had been left severely shocked.

The school made no acknowledgment that there could be any connection between breaking rules and this kind of experience. Nick— though appreciating his father's understanding—became increasingly disaffected and difficult at school and his work temporarily suffered badly. Had a teacher been more sympathetic at the time to his particular predicament and less rule bound in their response, Nick's school life might have suffered a great deal less.

The role of learning

There is a potentially huge expansion occurring at this stage in the range of ways of thinking and learning, of gathering information and acquiring technical skills. Because this expansion comes at the very time when so many other aspects of life are in flux, school activities often become an important barometer for how other things are going. Not that there is any kind of crude correlation between work difficulties and emotional difficulties. Indeed there is often an inverse relationship. For example, many parents will be aware that their child may be doing many hours of homework, less out of the joy of learning than out of worry about the more turbulent areas of their personal and social life.

In a general way, however, in the midst of the turmoil, some learning still seems to go on, and the intellectual growth that can occur at this time has a very important part to play in these young peoples' sense of themselves and their place in the world; in the discovery of new capacities and interests and in the promotion of self esteem. Learning may also often function as another source of contact between individuals, though that aspect would perhaps seldom be admitted. Looking back to this time, seventeen-year-old Jonathan commented, "The general line was always to complain about work. Although kids moan about school, you do learn and become interested. School actually becomes a place you want to be and home, after a couple of days, can be a bit boring. Though few would admit it, they are often thinking 'actually this is something I wouldn't mind learning about.' They don't speak about it but they do think, 'this is basically OK.'"

Many parents might be surprised to hear older teenagers agreeing with Jonathan's remark. In retrospect, many felt that they wished their school had a tighter grip on them and had offered more encouragement to keep working at this stage. They felt that their friends tended to take over in not altogether welcome ways, and that their work suffered, adding to the strains of the exams to come. This would not have been a view that many would have volunteered at the time, though some remembered becoming disaffected because they were bored or not sufficiently stretched. For them, feeling "in the doldrums' seemed to be related to frustrations in learning and "getting on.'

For some, the new kind of work pressures at this age have their stressful side and produce conflicts, stirring up competitiveness, fear of failure or excessive perfectionism which, if they are also expressions of other kinds of problem, may feel unmanageable at times. For others, that same pressure may enable them to begin to be aware of their capacities and strengths and to open up new worlds of interest and curiosity which strengthen their developing personalities and are ripe for encouragement. It is indeed difficult for parents neither to handicap their children by over-protection nor to harden or damage them by over-exposure. School now seems a world of its own, but parental involvement, encouragement and interest may be much more important than is apparent. The stresses of this group life are immense and may spill over in disruptive ways into the family. A sympathetic awareness of the nature of the struggles may, as always, play a crucial part in the young people's ability to get through them.

CHAPTER FOUR

GROUPS

One of the most common responses of twelve to fourteen year-olds to the stresses and uncertainties of school life, to the loosening of family bonds and to the confusion of feelings about themselves is to seek out the company of friends. At this age the groups of friends are of the utmost importance. In terms of whether they are going well or badly, they could be said, for the majority, completely to dominate the experience of school life. They serve several functions, often different for boys than for girls. Part of the agony for twelve year-olds, and perhaps for girls in particular, is that they may not yet have firmly established a group to which they can securely belong. They suffer, rather, almost daily betrayals, disloyalties, exclusions, hopes, disappointments which are often very hard to bear or to forgive. But by thirteen or fourteen the groups may have taken on an almost tribal significance of a passion and intensity towards each other and a hostility or indifference towards adults which is sometimes difficult for parents to understand.

Usually in each school year there are several groups according to race, gender and class—often reproducing society's own divisions and hierarchies. There tends to be the "in" group and the "out" group, the "brainy ones," the "no-hopers," the "heads" and the "casuals," the elite and the despised, the envious and the envied, the "hard" and the "wimps."

Each school throws up its own particular pattern. But it is interesting that the fluidity of groups of twelve-year-olds, when they are perhaps most confused about where their identifications and allegiances will ultimately lie, tends to have all but stopped by thirteen. Comings and goings to any significant degree between groups is increasingly unusual. Sometimes an individual child belongs to more than one. In such a case it is very common for them to be doing totally different things, behaving differently, feeling differently, depending on which group they are with. They may be extremely worried about any members of the respective groups encountering one another (just as they may be resistant to encountering their parents when in the company of friends). There may be, for example, one group at school, and a different one at home, or elsewhere in the community. And these groups may have very little in common with one another. Membership of several different groups, none of which is in contact with the other, enables different aspects of the young adolescent's personality to be kept separate. As it becomes bearable for those aspects to be brought together in a more coherent way—so members of the respective groups may finally be allowed to come in contact with each other.

The grouping may also be a very large one—of fans of a particular sports team, for example. But whether large groups or small groups, the basic issues tend to be the same—membership is about a way of sorting out identity. At a time when relationships with parents may have become difficult or distant, groups are a means of finding security with others who have something important in common, whatever that may be. Aspects of character which are not yet acknowledged, or felt to be an ongoing part of a sense of identity, can nonetheless be bound together by the loose and invisible bonds of group membership. Groups thus become safe places in which different bits of one individual's personality may be played out—often bits which are felt to be difficult to integrate at this stage.

In a group which roughly coheres in terms of style, race, fashion and class, there will usually be one member who is tougher, one smarter, one more sensitive, one rather rash, one deprived—each in a crude sense standing for the tough, rash, clever, sensitive aspect of each individual. The simplistic early stereotyping attributed to each member of "The Beatles" would be a case in point: John, clever, rash; Paul, sensitive; George, follower, less brilliant; Ringo, deprived.

In so far as everyone will at times feel, as Jane said, "completely misunderstood and a total outsider," the forces which bind this age group to an experience of similarity and belonging are usually very powerful ones. Approval and status within the group become all-important. Treachery and betrayal are agonizing. The individual groupings often themselves become mini-societies of competitiveness and status-seeking but not so intensely as to threaten the group as a whole. That is, these ambitious, disruptive, co-operative, dependent, or destructive impulses can, to a large extent be lived out and experimented with within the secure confines of the group structure.

This is often a great strain. Many feel the stress of maintaining membership of the group on the one hand and, on the other, feeling that "it was a burden keeping up with who they thought I was—marvelous, attractive, desirable. I felt I couldn't let them down and turned to diary-writing as the only place I could really be myself and express my worries." This comment of fourteen- year-old Anna would have surprised her friends who believed her to be the life and soul of any party. But perhaps each of them would have harbored some private recognition of what she was talking about. For it is partly to combat the fear of isolation and the stress of keeping up appearances that close friendships are formed in the first place.

In junior high school, friendship networks do tend to be the center of everybody's existence. They are felt to be the key to self-esteem, to a sense of identity. Nothing is more important than social life—whether it is actually happening or not—and much deeper feelings of distress and anxiety may be masked by the day-to-day "crises" of group membership. Gina, whose parents separated soon after her thirteenth birthday, described how nothing was more important than what was going on at school at the time. "Whether I'd snubbed someone or even whether I had the right jeans to wear seemed much more important than the fact that my parents were splitting up. . . .Work wasn't important," she continued, "it was school, socially, that counted, *nothing* else mattered."

Parents may be dismissed by the hitherto most loving of children; the activities of the group become paramount. Teachers too, even the most sympathetic, tend to be found irrelevant and embarrassing. A art teacher described his experience: "From regarding me as 'God' in the ninth grade, to thinking the 'world' of me in the tenth, in the eleventh *everything* I did was wrong and despicable. It was not until the twelfth grade that I became accepted again as a friend and teacher for whom they seemed to have some respect."

The pleasures of group life

The work side of things tends also to be dismissed at this stage. It interrupts social life. The importance of continuing to study runs counter to the intense internal and external pressures of the age group to find ways socially of sorting out who they are. Gossip prevails. It becomes essential information about the actions of others. In many households parents will find the telephone monopolized as soon as school is over. The seemingly endless (and expensive) appetite for conversations about each other's feelings, reactions and activities are often ways of trying out different aspects of themselves and others' reactions to them. The subject of the gossiping, in other words, may often represent experimental versions of themselves, and thus be inexhaustibly fascinating.

It is also essential to be at *all* the parties, as much in order not to have missed them, or not to have missed the post-mortem, as for the actual pleasure of being there. This is the time when such pressures are most strongly felt, the conflict between work and relationships most painful and the fights with parents about homework and leisure most violent. Parents find limits harder and harder to set as the social demands to be part of the scene intensify. Only a few months later, at the beginning of the twelfth grade, the conflict has often, to some extent, resolved—either to join those who are going to on to university or those who are not. But at this slightly younger age clothes, hair, music, image, appearance and above all, acceptance, are the main concerns.

Nadine was sent to the principal's office because she'd been caught smoking on school grounds. When he came out of his office to the waiting area the principal encountered six identically dressed fourteen year-olds wearing 501 jeans and Doc Marten boots. "We just wanted her to know that we are behind her," one of them said.

While being full of the kinds of anxiety described, fourteen year-olds often feel happier than twelve year-olds, no longer so confused about friends and identity, nor too worried about the pairing off into couples which tends to begin a bit later. They are still relatively free of anxieties about exam pressures or the what-am-I going-to-do-with-my-life worries that are to follow. The pains and pleasures of the fighting, talking, sharing, sub-grouping, excluding, re-grouping, all take place within a "holding" group structure—an alternative to the family which may never be quite as tight or relatively carefree again. Many fourteen year-olds face the coming year with fear and dread. The party is felt to be over.

Gangs

Not all twelve to fourteen year-olds, of course, find their way into these sorts of groups. The kind I have described are quite benign and co-operative, taking care of one another and feeling considerable mutual concern as well as competitiveness. Very different are the kinds of groups whose attitudes and activities make them more like gangs. Very different too is the young person who finds him or herself a member of neither group nor gang but on their own, perhaps not close to either family or friends.

In contrast to Nadine's group of friends, other combinations of twelve to fourteen year-olds may take on characteristics which are much less constructive—of tyranny and submission, of rebellion and criminality. They may have got together to express the destructive aspects of their personalities for the purposes of doing harm rather than for doing good. All groups at times exert pressure on their members to do things they would not have done as individuals. But that is a different matter from falling in with others *because* they seem to represent the more timid or vicious parts of the personality and to reproduce an atmosphere of fear and oppression, so attractive to those who have been intimidated and oppressed themselves.

"I couldn't count on friends for anything but trouble," said Jack, looking back to how he was "seduced" into his thirteen-year-old gang. "I started hanging around with this group . . . one of them had come up to me and said, 'You're cool, we like your looks,' and I just felt good for the first time and appreciated and wanted to be friends. But they started doing things I didn't really want to do—like skipping school and homework and I found myself going along with it even though I felt it wasn't me."

We can see from this that Jack was already vulnerable—he didn't feel good about himself. Feeling accepted and having friends whom he thought appreciated him, albeit only for his "hard" aspects, at least provided some kind of "home." Despite resistance, Jack found himself being pulled down a road he neither valued nor wanted. He lived in fear of being caught, or of being found out by his parents and "abandoned" as a result.

Jack's gang, as so often, was dominated by a couple of older boys, "leaders," who were felt to be charismatic, who "acted cool," and were already "into drugs and sex." These two offered the younger or weaker boys either the possibility of identifying with them—becoming sort of clones and tyrannizing other gangs—or becoming victims within their own group. Any steps towards leaving the gang invited harsh punishment. Jack managed to get out when his older brothers told his parents what was happening and they realized how unhappy and frightened Jack had been, and the extent to which, out of fear, he had been lying about his activities. Several years later, Jack had difficulty believing that the so-called leaders could ever have had such a hold on him. "They were really just victims themselves—and what is more, they haven't ever really changed. They're just the same now as they were then. They never grew up."

Isolation

Jack's younger sister, Sandra, was among those who, for temperamental, practical or even geographical reasons, are much more isolated. I have been generalizing about this age group but, of course, development runs at different speeds for different children. Some stick closer to the family for longer than others, remaining identified with parents' values and attitudes and preferring not to break out or run risks. Others are not in a position to spend much time with friends and may seek a different kind of companionship, for example, with pets, with books, film characters, or often privately, with toys that have usually been discarded by this age. This tendency to be alone may or may not be something to worry about. If it happens by choice, it may represent a degree of self-knowledge about when the child himself or herself is ready to set out and start making discoveries. It may, on the other hand, express anxiety about growing up, an avoidance of confusion and conflict, a kind of escape which expresses itself as lethargy, and which another child may seek in other forms of avoidance—alcohol or drugs, for example.

Isolated behavior may, as in Sandra's case, reflect a specific set of family stresses and needs. She was the baby of the family, particularly small for her age and always a poor eater. Sandra wanted to remain "in the nest," safe from the terrible dangers which she perceived as lying outside. She tended to stay at home whenever possible, watching television and not apparently interested in anything. Once she had transferred to junior high school her mother could no longer look after her and without the protection of a group, or of the sort of gang which her brother had joined, to give herself a sense of being someone, she was cruelly bullied. Sandra had started with a disadvantage—in being smaller than the others she *looked* different and thereby missed out on an important qualification for group membership—sameness. It may be, too, that her mother, in wishing to keep from her the more painful aspects of life, had actually denied her some of the capacities she needed to survive what has been called the "blackboard jungle."

The long periods of lethargy and apparent boredom which many twelve to fourteen year-olds seem to slide into, often involving videos, television, or computer games, may convey a kind of mindlessness which parents find very upsetting. The bright and enthusiastic young eleven-year-old seems to have "gone stupid." This is very likely to represent a period of withdrawal from engaging with the immediate conflicts, but it should always be taken seriously. The "doldrums" can also be an expression of deeper depression or avoidance, for which more than friendly tolerance may be required such as help from a counselor or therapist. Some children are so afraid of their anger and greed that without learning the confidence to express them in a situation where they can be understood and managed, they hardly know they exist.

Sandra was always surrounded by people well able to express strong negative feelings but she did not feel safe enough to do so herself. Thus she never really learned to look after herself. It may also be that her reluctance to eat was, as so often, linked with psychological difficulties of taking in experiences of which she was basically afraid, but which might have helped her stick up for herself a bit more effectively.

Parents will rightly feel anxious about whether their children seem to have found their way to a relatively constructive group of friends, who will support the curious, courageous and creative aspects of their characters, or whether the reverse may be true. For the groups or gangs of these early teenage years often have a lasting impact on attitudes, achievements and ways of life. Group or gang membership usually reflects aspects of the twelve to fourteen year-olds' personalities which can seldom be simplified as, "He fell in with the wrong crowd," or "She was lucky with her group of friends." Understanding the kinds of issues which underlie the complex allegiances involved may help to encourage the good characteristics and modify the bad.

CHAPTER FIVE

A QUESTION OF IDENTITY

Discovering "who am I?"

Part of the adolescent process being undertaken by the twelve to four-teen year-old is one which involves feelings they don't like, find painful or would wish to be without. All of us adopt a variety of ways of deal-ing with such feelings, but they are particularly in evidence in these early adolescent years. Many of what seem the most bemusing, incom-prehensible, destructive, disturbing (or even conforming) aspects of adolescence can be thought of as ways of attempting variously to cope with, bypass, deny, or get rid of painful and distressing experiences, often under the illusion that if they are not being directly felt or expressed, they are not really there.

What it feels like

More pain than is often realized attaches to the grief about leaving familiar things—the relative safety and certainty of childhood, the known and the recognizable—and moving towards an unknown future where every step of the way may feel both like a new ordeal, and, simultaneously, a new adventure. At the heart of this is the difficulty of leaving parents and home—though often not recognized as such. This may suggest an excessively rosy version of childhood. To those for whom the early years have been unhappy ones, adolescence may pose a welcome alternative and childhood be relinquished with scarcely a second thought. It is true that for some adolescence offers a second opportunity to engage with experiences and possible developments which were not available earlier, whether for reasons of health, loss, separation, or other problems.

Central to both the pain and the adventure for twelve to fourteen year-olds is the necessity of sorting out who they really are, as distinct from who parents think they are or would like them to be. The question of identity becomes the central issue. "Who am I?" Experimentation may be both a way of avoiding pain and a way of trying to establish who one is. The testing and challenging, both of adult authority and of themselves, tends to be at its most intense at this time. Thirteen-year-old Steven asked his mother one day, "Does everyone in the world think that they're the main guy?" This touchingly simple question was essentially about trying to understand himself. But it was also an expression of the dawning awareness of not being as special as he thought he was; everyone else might believe themselves to *be* just as special; might even be just as special. If you lose confidence in that kind of specialness how do you sort yourself out from the rest? The predicament becomes one of both wanting to be different and fearing to be different, or of wanting to manage to be different within recognizable boundaries. The courageous thrusts forward are usually, at this stage, accompanied by anxious pullings back. Parents may feel perplexed by this apparent inconsistency, yet also perhaps recognize it, for it may mirror their own mixed feelings about wanting both to push their children forward to grow up quickly, and to hold them back, mindful of "the day when they will be gone."

Rebelling and conforming

Again, early feelings may be stirred up, reminiscent of the toddler who ventures just out of sight one minute, only to rush anxiously back to base the next; and of the mother who both wishes her baby weaned and regrets the loss of the intimacy of breast-feeding; or of the father who feels the baby is driving a wedge between himself and his wife and seeks to regain the earlier equilibrium. Of course such feelings may vary enormously according to the place the child has in his or her particular family. The twelve year-old who has two older brothers or sisters may experience what feels like a very different mother from theirs. It is important to keep these earlier childhood experiences in mind since the way in which the stresses of adolescence are managed is often closely related to whether the impact of earlier difficulties has been understood in the past. For example, were child and parent able to express their feelings, and to some extent resolve them, at times of tension and anxiety? Extremes of behavior, whether conformity or delinquency, which appear as excessive reactions to the normal stresses of adolescence, often relate to earlier problems or traumas, the nature of which was not sufficiently acknowledged or understood.

Thirteen-year-old Katie had always been thought of as a "model child." Shortly before a piano exam, she suddenly started having panic attacks. She would run breathless and shaking from the room for no apparent reason. Six months earlier her little sister had been badly hurt in a car accident. Katie's mother had been deeply upset and depressed ever since, looked after mainly by Katie herself, who tried to "mother" her and cheer her up by efforts to be good.

It emerged that behind the good-girl exterior—and almost certainly related to the panic attacks—lay a terrible and long-standing fear of actually being very bad, even wicked; of having caused terrible happenings by her competitiveness and desire to be her mother's only one, and forever struggling (and necessarily failing) to compensate with her goodness.

Katie felt she was somehow impersonating someone she was not, covering up feelings of grief and guilt through conforming to what she felt was wanted, at the expense of her own identity. Her own distress had been insufficiently acknowledged because her mother was herself too upset to be able to help. Having expressed her anxieties, however, Katie had a second chance to try to come to terms with painful feelings, but this time with a school counselor, someone slightly removed from the situation and therefore better able to bear some of her emotions.

Katie, like Mary and Sandra, had particular motives for conforming. Others conform because, for whatever reason, they are happier that way—too timid, perhaps, to want to break away, too aware of parental distress were they to try to do so, too content where they are. Each child will have their own particular pace of development and for some the experimenting and challenging does not happen until a bit later. For others it may take covert and less recognizable forms.

Experimenting and testing: music, clothes, leisure

More common at this age, however, is the desire to test everyone and everything. Discovering what is "not me" is a very important step in sorting out what is me. It is often difficult for parents to understand that the fact that they themselves are being questioned and found wanting is only part of the story. What feels like rebelliousness, rejection and, occasionally, outright cruelty, may be an anxious expression of the need to find some kind of self-definition outside the family. It is often very hard for parents not to assume critical and superior attitudes towards these efforts at self expression, in much the same terms as they may be experiencing critical and superior attitudes from their children towards themselves.

The twelve to fourteen year-old is moving from being defined by, and defining themselves as, the son or daughter of their parents, to seeking to know who they are, as distinct from their parents. Concerns about the relationship between being a son or daughter and being a separate self become very insistent. For this reason, early adolescence is often the time when searching questions are raised about natural parents. Adolescents in their families of birth struggle with tolerating and integrating (or rejecting) the clues and pointers they encounter every day.

Adopted children and their adoptive parents face particular difficulty when the question, "Who am I?" is being asked, with far fewer clues or pointers. At least to be able to question, accept or discard these clues is a position in itself. Not having them, the adopted child has to cope with not knowing what is felt to be crucial information about themselves, and having to accommodate the idea of at least two sets of parents. This situation can feel very confusing and lonely, for young adolescents in particular. They may find themselves going to greater and greater extremes in their need to test themselves and, especially, their adoptive parents' love for them, in an attempt to find some kind of secure and meaningful basis for their own sense of self.

Taste in music is often the first casualty of shared family life—music expressing the *differently* primitive sounds and group allegiances of a *different* pattern, in a *different* generation. Pearl Jam to the present parental generation may seem vastly inferior to the Beatles or Eagles—"Where's the tune, where are the lyrics?" "I'll go mad if that bass goes on thumping a minute longer." But the choice of popular music, whether acid, rap, reggae, hip hop or rock, is a reflection of a youth culture of a very contemporary kind, racially mixed as perhaps never before, immediate, real and belonging to *them*, not to us—part of the initiation into the tribe.

Clothes may be closely allied to the music—again to do with statements of difference and belonging, with group identity and with ritual behavior. The longing for difference from parents and authority figures, the seeking after new mentors, is a necessary but risky business, the uncertainty of which is often expressed in the tendency to wear the same clothes. This may also be, in part, an attempt to cover up actual differences and seek similarities, but it is also a manifestation of the very serious commitment to group life already described.

There are often seemingly incongruous expressions of the desire to dress differently from parents. In one somewhat unconventional family, the father characteristically wore dirty jeans and shoulder-length hair. His fourteen year-old son's response was to iron his jeans, wear a white shirt and tie and sandals. The effect was just as intended—his father was uncomprehending and furious.

The shared impulse tends to be to try to live on the edge. Boys' increased physical strength and energy encourages them to test their own daring and prowess to the limit. Their sporting activities may often take them to the end of their physical endurance. At this age the important issue is often the process itself and not the goal. Activities such as basketball, football, mountain biking, surf boarding, for example, become, for boys in particular, a passion. If these activities are a response to parental indifference or adopted in a spirit of rebellion against excessive parental restraint, they may give expression to desperate urges to escape, to override, to challenge, to cry for help, to create a crisis—particularly clear if accidents begin regularly to occur.

It is also true, of course, that in the male world, and to a lesser degree in the female, sporting activities offer a continuing bond of excitement and shared interest which can surpass divides of generation, class, race and sexual difference. Sons, and increasingly daughters, may communicate with parents across players' stats and play-offs in a way that is hardly imaginable in any other area of their respective lives.

Moreover, in other states of mind, daring deeds and athletic feats may have less to do with excitement and danger, or with engendering anxiety in others, than with a wish to discover the relationship between aspiration and realization. Parents need to have the confidence themselves to let their children run risks, make mistakes, suffer the consequences, but within a firm boundary of known and negotiated limits.

Other areas of "leisure" activity may prove far more problematic: "What do you want?" screamed the distraught mother of fourteen-year-old Rosie, who had been sleeping out with a group of friends for several nights without telling her parents where she was. "To do what I want, without you," was the furious reply. "Well you can't. You at least have to call us." The negotiation was eventually and painfully concluded. If Rosie stayed out she would always let her parents know where she was. If she asked to be picked up they would come for her. If she wished to walk after 11:00 PM it would never be with fewer than two other friends.

Going to the limits

Both Rosie and her friend Emily spent their years from 12-14 courting danger. They described, in retrospect, what a strain the seeking for status, the urge to *be* someone had been, whether through sex, drugs, appearance or recklessness. They said that they had somehow believed that there would be guardian angels protecting them from the terrible risks they ran. They spoke, too, of what a relief it was to feel able, finally, at fifteen, to acknowledge their true "guardians," namely their parents, and to bring their friends home with the recognition that communication between generations was, after all, possible.

Emily described how awful it had been petting with boys when she was twelve. "I didn't want it, I didn't like it. I found it horrible, at the same time exciting, and I was supposed to want to do it. When I tried smoking and drugs I found them absolutely disgusting, but being grown-up meant doing these things which I hated and looking as though I was enjoying it."

Rosie and Emily were both painfully discovering something about what it meant to be themselves by experiencing what *wasn't* themselves.

They both described how, at the time, they would attach themselves to glamorous older boys who represented direct challenges, and also alternatives, to their parents. They sought status, flattered by the attention and by false promises ("I can get you into clubs free"; "I can get you a job any time"). Because girls, as we have seen, mature slightly earlier than boys, at this point they are often going out with partners two or three years older than themselves, thus finding themselves involved in activities, sexual experimentation in particular, which tend to be far more precocious than that of their male counterparts—both thrilling and terrifying.

Emily and Rosie described their girlfriends as either like themselves, "vamps" as they put it, or as trying to prolong their innocence by remaining "tomboys." Each type was putting off the dangerous moment of engaging with their actual femininity by identifying with caricatured aspects of the female and male worlds. Both of these strategies, they reflected, might have had something to do with trying to find alternatives to the main model of femininity that seemed available— that of "mother." Both these strategies also reflected very familiar ways in which girls either avoid, or prematurely engage with, what puberty thrusts upon them. These ways are often only temporary and, as with Rosie and Emily, have more or less passed by the time of adolescence proper. But, at the time, parents tend to feel tested to their limits—as they are meant to be.

Parents' response to the challenge

Parents often suffer the anxiety instead of the adolescent doing so.

They suffer it for them and have to find ways of being able to bear *not* knowing what is happening all the time, ways of perpetuating in their children the knowledge that their home remains their haven, albeit abused at times; ways of being able to face how much they *might* be hurt and worried if they knew what their children were doing and of not being frightened of that; ways of understanding that the "drama queen" or "cool cat" of today is still the frightened child of tomorrow, who is in danger of feeling completely misunderstood and cut off from home roots.

Crucial to parents' capacity to manage any of these taxing undertakings is the recognition on their part that straight prohibition is likely to engender either secret rebelliousness or cowardly submission, and that excessive tolerance usually initiates a search for limits on the part of the twelve to fourteen year-old, however far that may take them. Here past patterns of family authority may be very important. There is usually a world of difference, in terms of self regulation in young adolescent behavior, between authority that is based on love and authority that is based on fear. An aspiration towards realizing their capacities that is based on love is a great deal nearer to the possibility of being truly themselves than one based on fear. The latter threatens with failure, with falling below standards, with not fulfilling some parental promise rather than their own promise.

One young graduate from an uneducated but very ambitious background, having just graduated from a first-class university, recalled his toil and effort at getting where he was. "That's the last thing I'll ever do for my father," he said. And only then was he able to begin the now belated, and therefore more painful, task of sorting out who he really was—apart from being a clever boy and a successful son.

CHAPTER SIX

RUNNING INTO DIFFICULTIES

The previous chapter described the normal testing, differentiating and limit-finding that often, though by no means always, characterizes the 12 to 14 age group. Any one of these routes to self discovery may extend into more worrying behavior if it goes beyond what is tolerable to the young adolescent or parent, the school or wider community. It may find expression in behavior or in states of mind that are anti-social, delinquent, seriously self damaging and destructive, or in some sense out of control.

The urge to self discovery is likely, as we have seen, to be to do with separation from parents, conflicts, losses, disappointments, and with finding out who one is and what one wants. But although it is characteristic of this age to go to extremes, problems may arise when ordinary and appropriate exploration goes too far. The difficulty often presents itself as not knowing where to draw the line, or how to recognize the crossover point from "extreme" to "abusive," whether of computer games, food, drugs, alcohol, sex, work or whatever.

This is a particularly difficult area for parents since it usually stirs up powerful feelings. Anger, shame, guilt or distress often make it hard to see that such abuses, whether directed at the young adolescents themselves, the parent or the outside world, may also be important forms of communication, though the true message may have become obscure.

If the communication aspect can be grasped, some kind of understanding and containment of the problem may be achieved. The difficulty is that by its very nature this more extreme behavior tends to obliterate thought and meaning and to focus instead on action and reaction. The greater freedom, independence and responsibility that young people begin to acquire at twelve, however much desired, often make problems and decisions seem overwhelming. "I can get so depressed," said John, "part of me knows I can get out of it really, but I also don't want to. I sort of enjoy it. I suppose I really want my mom to come and look after me." Feelings such as these can be so intense that the only thing to do seems to be to act, or "act out," as it is sometimes called. The "acts" are responses to inner pain, often related to external and understandable stresses. But just as often they appear not to be attached to any obvious source. Many twelve to fourteen year-olds don't know why they feel the way they do and then feel worse because there is no apparent reason. Often the world seems suddenly and unexpectedly bleak. Equally suddenly a small change may transform everything.

After a particularly intense outburst of bad temper, thirteen-year-old Carol admitted to feeling depressed—she had no idea why. Nothing was going right for her and she felt really bored. A few minutes later the postman brought a special magazine she had sent away for. Her face lightened and she completely cheered up. "I think maybe I was just disappointed because my mag hadn't arrived."

Much more significant is when it is not the magazine but the friend who doesn't arrive, or turns out to be spending the day with someone else despite a prior arrangement, or when your child doesn't get invited to a party that everyone else is going to. The capacity at this age to deal with these kinds of setbacks or disappointments depends on a number of things which have a lot to do with how serious a risk there may be of damaging or destructive behavior as a result. First of all, puberty affects different children in different ways. Some experience a sudden and dramatic increase in their feelings of anger and aggression as well as of passion and desire, and have impulses they find very hard to control. For others the situation is much less intense or disturbing. The capacity to manage these new feelings, of whatever intensity, has a great deal to do with the degree of understanding communication about emotional states and their expression which exists in a family. Some children feel that their parents are able to think about and respond appropriately and wisely to child-like struggles to communicate. They have learned to expect their feelings to be "held" when they have not been able to do so themselves. In this way they will have had the opportunity to develop that same capacity in themselves. They will be able to think before they act, in turn to "hold" extremes of feeling, without lashing out or being overcome by them.

This past capacity on the parents' part is often for the first time sorely tested in young adolescence. The childrens' impulses are particularly strong. One way of dealing with them may be to try to get rid of feelings into someone else, either to get others to feel them instead, or to communicate just how horrible the feelings are. If parents are still able to acknowledge, tolerate and relate sympathetically to these, by turn, adult and infantile explosions of rage, love, despair, dependency, they will stand their children in better stead for establishing their own limits. The children will feel additionally strengthened or supported in the holding of their own line if there is felt to be a measure of parents' trust in their ability to do just that. Enormous self respect accrues from the knowledge that parents basically believe in their children and will back them.

This should not be confused with a family position that is so tolerant that anything goes, or so intolerant that blind loyalties obscure more subtle differentiations about right and wrong. Children of such parents are often exposed to particular difficulties in controlling their behavior and impulses because they have no wise internal rules (or guardian angels) to fall back on. They may become either excessively guilt-ridden and hard on themselves, struggling both with their need to indulge feelings and with their self hatred in so doing, or they may become excessively punitive and vengeful with unthinking responses of the "eye for an eye" variety.

It is the parent who is able to discriminate between, say, need and greed, between what really matters and what doesn't, and is prepared to hold out for what they believe is right despite a fight, who can help engender in the children a similar capacity—extremely important to try to maintain in adolescence, even if it seems a bit ragged at the edges at times.

Families in which parents find it difficult to control their own impulses, or ones in which excesses or inconsistencies of whatever kind are a characteristic of home life, often find that their young adolescent also has difficulties with self control—either too much or too little. Similarly, excessively rigid and authoritarian households, who tend to see things in very polarized ways may, inadvertently, encourage their children to go to extremes, while believing that what they are doing is setting limits.

It is between the ages of twelve and fourteen, when the bodily changes are greatest and the consequent emotions and relationships most new, exciting and frightening, that these internal controls become most severely tested and, as a result, pose particularly demanding challenges to outsiders—to family life and school life above all. It is not surprising that the peak age for "acting out" of all kinds is fourteen.

Stealing

Susan, fourteen, had been stealing again. The recent incident came to light when her teacher questioned her mother about the inappropriately expensive clothes and jewelry she was wearing to school. The teacher felt concerned rather than punitive because she knew that Susan had been unhappy for some time and had discussed with her whether or not she would like to talk to a counselor about her behavior. The teacher's attitude encouraged Susan to share her feelings. The recent theft of money from her grandmother (with which she had bought the clothes) was more serious than in the past when she'd taken minor items or small sums of money from her mother. When Susan said she had also taken the blame for a friend's recent theft, the teacher realized that Susan had probably *wanted* to be found out, which was why she had worn the fruits of her pickings so ostentatiously at school.

She put this to Susan who agreed and then tearfully poured out the story of the last few years. It had begun when her mom's boyfriend had unexpectedly moved in two years before. Her own father having died four years before that, Susan now felt that she had lost both her parents and she wasn't central in anyone's life. Her moodiness around the house and her frank sexual competitiveness with her mother for the boyfriend had raised threats to put her in foster care. She acknowledged that she was pushing her mother to the limit and trying to drive a wedge in the relationship between her and the new boyfriend, but said she felt she couldn't help it. When her mother had turned to a boyfriend instead of to her to help get over her grief for her dead husband, Susan had just felt despairing—no one understood or could bear *her* needs. She felt very angry and abandoned and had considered suicide in a vengeful kind of "then she'll be sorry" way, but "for some reason," she said, "I ended up stealing instead."

The teacher suggested that Mom and her boyfriend come in to school and that they all talk about it together. Mother was upset to learn how very unhappy Susan had been. She had attributed Susan's bad behavior to jealousy of her boyfriend and had hoped that she would grow out of it. She said that Susan had not grieved for her father much at the time and she thought she'd got over it—acting as a tower of strength towards her mom, rather than showing any great distress herself. Mom described herself as feeling too overcome to notice much at the time anyway.

It became possible to talk not only about Susan's jealousy, which was certainly strong, but also about the much deeper feelings of underlying grief and loss. She had tried to overcome these feelings initially by looking after her mother as the only way that she felt she could get looked after herself—that is, she did for her mother what she felt *she* needed. But when the boyfriend took over that role Susan felt she had nothing to offer. She described competitiveness, anger and even hatred towards her mother, the very person whom she also loved so profoundly. This made her guilty and terribly confused. Moreover, just at the point when she herself was sexually maturing, her mother had found a new boyfriend. Susan explained how she felt really put down by that, and anxious about whether *she* would ever be found attractive or have a boyfriend of her own.

The stealing could thus be thought of as a way of getting back from her mother and grandmother something she believed she had lost and should rightfully be hers. It could also be thought of as a way of acquiring things relating to the very area she was anxious about—items of femininity with which she sought to boost her "image" and attract the boys. The stealing had a third function for Susan. She hoped that punishment would relieve her feelings of guilt—not about the stealing itself, but about her aggressive impulses towards her mother and her mother's relationship.

The stealing was, then, a distress signal—one which Susan had to escalate when the initial salvoes went unnoticed. Fortunately, in this case, her teacher was sufficiently understanding to "read" the stealing for what it was. Having been able to talk over her feelings of rage and guilt, Susan no longer felt compelled to act in such a way as to invite a punishment that would be quite irrelevant to the crime.

Stealing can be taken to stand for a whole range of so-called anti-social acts with which parents of twelve to fourteen year-olds so often find themselves involved. The challenging or "naughty" behavior often arouses punitive impulses and sterner discipline is felt to be the solution. But there is usually an underlying reason based in conflict or distress. Understanding what the problematic behavior may mean, and being able to sort out the appropriate response may be difficult if you are closely involved and feelings are running high. Often the views of a thoughtful third person, like the teacher in this case, will be helpful in knowing the best way to proceed.

Drinking, drugs and other problems

Drinking, and experimenting with other substances, whether solvents or drugs, is another illegal and difficult area which a large number of parents reluctantly find themselves having to face—in terms of their fears for their young, of what they feel about it and of what they are going to do about it. As with stealing, this kind of problem may have a number of meanings. Having some sense of what it may be about in relation to a particular child is much more helpful than a cover-all response based on anxiety, prohibition or possibly ignorance.

As we have seen, the onset of adolescence may be felt to be "too much" and drinking or taking substances is one of the many forms of running from it that are adopted—quick solutions to painful problems. It is very difficult, especially now that drugs are so easily available, to resist the temptation to avoid the unpleasant or imperfect aspects of life by escaping into altered states of mind, in which the world may look more manageable. The desire to take drugs is often based on wanting to avoid pain and conflict. It may also have to do with the adolescent yearning for new experiences, with the belief that it will lead to important self discoveries. It can have to do with not wanting to be different from the group who are beginning to experiment; or it may be simply for status. It may, like many kinds of criminality and delinquency, be an omnipotent source of excitement about being powerful, without having to go through the painful process of acquiring a sense of strength and influence by slower and more ordinary means. Defying normal social rules often offers great social status among other adolescents and taking drugs, in particular, seems related to the desire to seem "cool" and grown-up.

A helpful parental response to this alarming world might initially be simply to know the facts, to have some sense of the respective dangers and effects of different drugs, to be able both to recognize worrying signs and to distinguish between situations in which there should be legitimate alarm or a more permissive attitude.

Fourteen-year-old Sarah, who had been smoking her older sister's cannabis for over a year, described watching a TV program on teenage drug habits with her parents. Her mother had commented, "What must these parents be like? If that was you, we'd know." It had never crossed these parents' minds that either of their daughters knew anything about drugs. Or perhaps they had never allowed themselves to be aware of the signs. Whatever the reason, this ignorance on their part was for the girls, in the short term, a source of relief, tinged with triumph. Later, however, when their habit escalated to harder drugs and eventually came to light, Sarah and her sister found themselves without any basis of family understanding or support, either for their addictive behavior or for the difficulties which underlay it. The family exploded in rage and grief and only then did the painful process begin of discovering and facing the reality of their relationships.

Drinking or experimenting with drugs may, on the other hand, also be part of a rather more constructive self exploration, and a way of questioning the conventions of family and society—"How can you think drugs are so terrible when you poison yourself with cigarettes and alcohol every day?" This attitude may characterize those who are not so much self destructive or escapist as going through a period of challenging rules as a necessary step towards accepting them. They are seeking, in other words, to come to conclusions based on their own experience rather than because their parents told them so. Many of the arguments a twelve to fourteen year-old will mount with their parents are really arguments with themselves—wanting the saner and more reasonable self to be supported and understood, despite protest. As such, they represent a statement of conflict—one part desiring the very discipline that the other part is busy flouting.

The drug culture is a terrifying one for any parent of teenage children. Many parents will have learned to their cost that "prohibition" really spells "invitation" and that in this area, as now in so many, their children cannot in any straightforward sense be controlled. Beyond the necessary explanations of the risks and dangers, parents have to think about what their own attitude really is. They have to be mindful of what their own "drug" behavior may signify to their children—tobacco, alcohol, sleeping pills, tranquilizers. And they have to reflect on what drugs may mean, for their own child in particular, in terms of the variety of motives and possibilities described above.

Mrs. Green phoned her friend in a panic. Her husband had come home recently at an unexpected hour and found their fourteen-year-old son, Jonathan, smoking a joint with a couple of friends. What should she do? "I know he's a bit of a terror and we had to be pretty heavy with him about cigarettes when he was twelve, but I thought he'd stopped smoking—and anyway this is a very different thing." She said that she had forbidden him ever to touch the stuff again but wasn't at all sure that he would abide by that. Two months later another mother called to complain to Mrs. Green that Jonathan had been supplying his grade nine classmates with dope. "Where," she demanded, "did he get the money from?" It turned out that Jonathan received $10 a day as an allowance—no questions asked. While consciously appalled at the idea of their son taking drugs, the parents were at the same time supplying him with the means, without a thought for the impossible temptation that this might arouse in such a boy.

Like many areas of twelve- to fourteen-year-old activity and experimentation, the culture of drugs tends to be a secret one, largely conducted "underground" and without parents' knowledge—in itself, of course, an important source of attraction and excitement. Degrees of involvement with drugs vary enormously at this age. Some will be forming a habit, others only rarely trying things out, and yet others having no such access or experience.

It is, then, a rare young person who, like Annie, explicitly raised her wishes and anxieties with her parents. Annie had become friendly with a group of fourteen year-olds who regularly took acid trips. She wanted to try herself but was worried because one of her friends had recently had a very frightening experience during a "trip." She took the very unusual step of asking her parents what they would think if she tried.

Annie's parents had quite a permissive attitude towards her older brothers occasionally smoking marijuana and they had a general but rather vague sense of the nature and effects of "acid" or L.S.D. Wisely, in response to Annie's question, they decided to find out more about the subject. What they discovered caused them considerable concern and they passed on to Annie the information they had acquired about the specific dangers and possible disturbing consequences of such a drug. In the course of this discussion Annie decided that, despite group pressure, she would resist the temptation and felt relieved to have her parents' thoughtful and informed position to support her.

Eating disorders

Drug-taking certainly falls into the category of what is called self abuse. Although this often involves both boys and girls alike at this stage, it tends to be the boys who find it harder to exercise restraint. An eating disorder, on the other hand, is primarily a girl's problem. Being self-conscious and health-conscious is an ordinary part of being adolescent. Many twelve year-olds, for example, of either gender become vegetarian at this age, driven by a variety of motives—ethical, political, economic. These motives are often underpinned by anxieties about contamination, cruelty and guilt which precisely connect to their unconscious preoccupations, however the conscious position may be rationalized.

But issues around food often take on a more troubling tone than the criticisms and well-argued positions on, for example, vegetarianism. Most twelve to fourteen year-olds feel dissatisfied with how they look—the boys no less than the girls. But whereas puberty for a boy tends to increase height, build, strength and energy, contributing to their sense of manliness and potency, for girls the picture is very different. For them puberty brings a filling out of the bodily contours, a roundedness of hips, a developing of breasts and a general weight gain. Their upward growth spurt tends to come earlier than that of boys. For many puberty tends to mean growing "out" rather than "up," filling many twelve year-old girls with fear and hatred of their new bodies, with anxiety about being fat and a determination to go on a diet.

The loss of the old shape and the unwilling change to the new also represents a definite shift from child to woman and the ending of the choice to be boyish, or tomboyish, which many girls make as preferable to being part of the world of girls and mothers. The fact that it is currently still fashionable for women to be thin makes things more difficult. Many girls begin to be worried about the amount of food, and the kind of food, they eat at this stage in ways that may become seriously problematic later. Many begin to starve, or to overeat. This may be a reaction to, or a compensation for, how bad they feel about themselves or a response to the loss of, or absence of, things they still feel they need but can no longer have. In a very simple sense starving (anorexia) can feel like a way of exerting control over a life that is feared to be becoming unmanageable in ways already described, or has been felt until now to be in the control of others (especially the mother).

Overeating (compulsive eating and, if accompanied by vomiting and taking laxatives, bulimia) by contrast, may represent both a feeling that things are out of control, and a desperate attempt to regulate that and to stop it before disaster strikes. Either over- or under-eating involves girls in a considerable amount of self hatred, the beginnings of which are often evident in this twelve-to- fourteen-year-old age group.

Again, taking too much food or refusing food, or developing food fads and weird diets almost always stirs up strong reactions in parents, particularly the mother, who feels either that she is being rejected, or that she cannot provide enough of the right things. She may find it hard to restrain irritation about apparently irrational and exacting food fads, for example, and to allow her daughter freedom in this area. For she, as mother, will often become aware that in relation to her own body and to her relationship to her maturing daughter, food is seldom a neutral topic. Unless a lot of understanding is brought to the situation it can become an agonizing battleground for other things: "I hate myself," is often dealt with on the part of the young girl by: "I hate you."

Promiscuity

Like eating disorders and drugs, promiscuity, long recognized as a problem for older adolescents, is becoming more common in the younger age group. Promiscuity at this age is clearly a self-destructive and risky way of expressing a variety of feelings—whether fear of separation, loneliness, self hatred, desperation, need for love, desire for danger, or desire for "adulthood," without the intervening uncertainty. These days it carries with it the specific and horrifying danger of AIDS. As we have seen, sexual experimentation can sometimes be part of young people's efforts to find out who they are, what they want and how they feel. If, however, it takes the form of sensual relationships with many partners but without apparently any intimate feelings or lasting commitments, probably there is a cry for help going on, whether the "child" knows it or not. Again, understanding what may underlie the behavior and how it relates to the parents' attitude to sexuality is of utmost importance.

Any of the activities and preoccupations of this age group may, of course, be taken to excess at any time. The reasons are usually similar: distress about feelings that your twelve to fourteen year-old does not understand clearly him or herself, nor believe that anyone else is able to do so, attempts to avoid having those feelings, and a sense that people who could have helped in the past are no longer able to—namely the parents. It is hard to accept that you may indeed no longer be the person they want to talk to—especially for a single parent. But it is, above all, the recognition of what these processes are about and the ability to let them be themselves, perhaps very different from you, or from what they think you want them to be, that may make all the difference.

In these difficult areas it is important for parents to be aware of their own states of mind at that age. Being able to be in some kind of dialogue with their own twelve- to fourteen-year-old selves, with the feelings of being young teenagers, can help enormously in understanding both their children and the nature of their own reactions to them.

Parents may often unexpectedly come across long-buried aspects of early experience which color their attitudes and influence their behavior towards their young. They may find themselves relating to their own teenager in precisely the ways their parents did to them. Remembering how they felt then may avoid simply repeating conflicts. They may then be able to free their children to find more enlightened ways of expressing themselves, encouraging independence within a sense of secure and caring limits. They may equally, on the other hand, find themselves too much in tune with the twelve- to fourteen-year-old reactions and lack the necessary parental distance which, though annoying, may also offer the teenager firm and helpful boundaries.

One can see how many of the problems which become serious in adolescence proper may have their roots in this age group. One can see, too, how important it is to understand what is going on at the time, lest the eating fads become disorders, lest the feelings about emptiness become ones of pointlessness, and despair and suicide threaten, lest the confusions and difficulties become forms of avoidance and mindlessness, lest the self hatred become serious self abuse, where self mutilation, drugs, sex, and numerous other forms of self destructiveness become the ways that some unhappy adolescents find to harm themselves and to distress others.

CHAPTER SEVEN

LIFE IN THE FAMILY

For the child, letting go of those who have been the center of the world for so long is a painful business. The cruelty or casualness with which it is often done may mask deep underlying distress. The person who until then has had most of the answers cannot now be looked to for solutions to, or opinions on, areas of anxiety and confusion that may feel more pressing and frightening than anything that has gone before. They cannot be looked to not only because, in reality they are not able to make everything all right in the way that they have in the past, but because to try to do so is to maintain an intimacy which is now felt to be threatening and unwelcome. One sad and disillusioned fourteen year-old reflected on his disappointment, "I realized they couldn't get me through life. I had to do it by myself."

The problem for the twelve-to-fourteen age group is that they feel a pull away from parents (particularly Mother) and back to them at the same time, and the various solutions they find to cope with this fact are not very firm or long-lasting. They find the inside conflicts hard to sort out, but they also become driven by outside social pressures to behave in ways which they may not really feel ready for. These muddles are often evident to parents in the young adolescent's characteristic desire to be allowed to remain childlike, having things done *for* them—room cleared up, breakfast made, etc.—while at the same time wanting the privileges of adulthood—staying up late, being given responsibility.

Fourteen-year-old Jason's mother was perplexed by his constant complaints that she was never home. She asked him why it was so important for her to be there when he himself was always out with his friends. "That's different," was his reply. "I just want you to be at home whether I'm there or not." What is often difficult to recognize is that it is precisely the mother-taking-care-of-son-at-home that frees him to explore areas of his life with his friends elsewhere. The security of feeling Mother is at home becomes a precondition for further experimentation.

For the first time, then, your children are likely to be going through a lot that you don't know about—and necessarily so. When you start encountering a new secretiveness and reserve it becomes painfully clear that they are definitely entering their own world. Their hopes and fears, anxieties and conflicts will increasingly become ones which they will often struggle with alone or with friends. Making it clear that you are available as and when they indicate that they wish to confide may be the best you can do. You may be both wanted and yearned for in your old role, as the one who is "there," yet felt to be useless, stupid, embarrassing, redundant, intrusive, as the one who has to be left. Some days, or even some moments, it will be one, and some the other. You may constantly have to remind yourself that one of the central tasks of this age group is to separate from you, and there is no predicting the ways and means in which this will be done.

Parents may find themselves thinking, "They've stopped needing me or talking to me in the way they used to, there's no point in my making an effort to be in after school or during the evenings." The child's response, like Jason's may well be, "But I want you to be there in case I need you." The point is simply to provide a stable background, or base from which the child can go out into the world. Finding the right balance between being experienced as intrusive on the one hand, or uninterested on the other, is very hard. The likelihood is that it is very important to be made to feel that you've got it wrong whatever you do. It is part of the struggle to separate, and to bear the pain of it, that what is being separated from has at times to be felt to be not worth having anyway. Parents are left with the feeling of being useless and helpless a lot of the time. The capacity to engender such feelings is particularly characteristic of twelve to fourteen year-olds. A little later the adolescent and parents may have found a way back to a relationship on a different basis, but at this stage it is a painful experience for parents both to be actively devalued, and perhaps to be discovered as not being what they thought they were.

Parents separating from children

Wounded parents are having to think hard about the unfairness of being ignored or harshly judged and wrong-footed at every turn on the one hand, and on the other, having to face actual deficiencies in themselves which they might otherwise prefer not to see or think about. The patterns of discipline and response which have become well-established within the family group may now be altered, disrupted, tested anew. Sticking to familiar patterns of authority is often found simply not to work anymore. Indeed those patterns themselves may now be revealed as obsolete, unjust or simply irrelevant.

The important thing is that we as parents have to be prepared to change too, and have to be able to deal with the adolescent in ourselves, perhaps alarmingly thinly covered over with what we took to be our mature, adult selves. Often the children will provoke fights to find out what we're *really* like. Often, too, no one likes what they find—least of all ourselves. They may reveal in us hypocrisy and double standards. We may have to acknowledge envy of their youth, beauty, and opportunities. We may have to face our own inability to let go or to separate, to allow them their freedom. For many this involves the painful acknowledgment that the "child" is no longer "theirs" in the way that the pre-pubescent child was felt to have been. Up until now you have made the rules, chosen the clothes, organized the activities, been the person turned to for approval, love, advice, comfort. All of a sudden, at thirteen or so, the child is felt no longer to belong to you—and this is extremely threatening to many parents. We may also feel threatened by fears of being surpassed, left behind and no longer needed. Parents of children this age may have to struggle with unexpected and disturbing possibilities, like the arousal of their own sexual desires towards their now physically maturing children.

Although seldom experienced consciously or explicitly, such feelings may often lie behind the intensity of parents' reactions and prohibitions—rational rules and strictures often ill-concealing more basic possessive and emotionally charged responses, the fundamental nature of which they may be unaware. There may, in other words, be many confusions in ourselves—inconsistencies, about-turns, which make the adolescent's task harder unless it can all be faced for what it is. Here a thoughtful partner or friend with whom to share the stresses and incomprehensions can be enormously supportive and reassuring, and help to contain some of the parents' more "adolescent" outbursts.

Separation and divorce

In a new family where either or both "parental" adults may have had children by former partners, or be beginning another young family of their own, the expression of feelings may take very extreme forms, especially if blame is being attributed by the grown-ups. Twelve to fourteen year-olds naturally see things in very exaggerated terms and tend to view the replacement partner through biased eyes, usually because they are *not* the real parent, but sometimes because the new partner may be felt to be better than the natural parent.

All the bad feelings they have but are frightened of expressing towards the natural parent may be directed towards the replacement. One parent thus becomes exaggeratedly good, with qualities perhaps valued beyond their actual worth, while the other becomes excessively devalued and criticized at every turn. The splits may be felt to be, indeed are, like those in the fairy tales—the wicked witch and the good fairy, the wicked stepmother and the good father. There is, of course, a tendency towards this kind of split between good and bad in any family with children of this age, but it is usually much more obvious and painful when separation has occurred or is threatening. This is especially hard for parents and new partners since so many raw nerves are likely to be being touched. But it is important both to take very seriously the hurt, and therefore often very hurtful feelings of the young person, and also to try to moderate them where possible, making efforts not to intensify them either by ignoring the distress or by adding fuel to the flames.

Ron was fourteen. His mother, though separated for five years, nonetheless felt very upset when her ex-husband began to live with a girlfriend, Joan, and she couldn't resist criticizing Joan at every opportunity. Ron had mixed feelings to start with. He was a bit relieved that his father was no longer on his own and that therefore he, Ron, didn't have to feel responsible for spending time with him and cheering him up. But as time went on he got more and more upset. His mom was upset, his dad was completely taken up with the new relationship and, worst of all, they were talking about having another baby. He started telling his mother that he was beginning to dislike Joan, then that he actually couldn't stand her, and finally that he totally hated her.

When he stormed home one night announcing that he absolutely refused to eat any food Joan cooked for him, his mother's feelings were very complicated. At one level she was delighted that Ron would not eat *her* food. But she also realized the danger of supporting him in that position. She felt it was too extreme, in that Joan really seemed like a nice young woman and was obviously trying to be good to the children. Was Ron wanting to please his mom? Feeling jealous and displaced by Joan? Furiously needing a reason to reject his father and doing so by rejecting the girlfriend? Or was he angrily expressing feelings about Joan which he was not able to admit to having about his mother? It may have been a mixture of all of these things and more.

Contrary to her own impulses, Ron's mom decided, that he should be encouraged to go on seeing his father, but perhaps not always with Joan there as well. It seemed to her that the most important thing was not to put at risk a relationship which was basically very important to Ron at a time when he was reacting quite violently to a number of other things, but to try, rather, to support him and his dad and see how things could develop from there. Part of Ron's difficulty may also have had to do with the fact that, seeing his father happy with another young woman, not his mother, stirred his feelings of grief about the actual separation five years ago. It is very common in this age group for feelings about loss and grief to be re aroused in this way, and often very painfully.

Such was the case with Mary. A few months before her fourteenth birthday she started crying inconsolably at the least provocation. Her friends were worried about her and told her home room teacher. Until then she had been a model student, an apparently popular and happy girl . To start with it was thought that she was both upset about her close friend leaving the school and worried about the academic tests she would have to take to gain entry to a prestigious high school. For she had already expressed anxiety about fulfilling her parents' academic expectations.

In conversation with her home room teacher, Mary poured out profound grief and distress about her parents' divorce six years earlier. The teacher had heard from Mother about the separation and had been told that Mary took it very well at the time, in fact had hardly seemed troubled by it at all. She had apparently immediately begun working hard and excelling at everything. Mary's present distress belied the optimistic and understandably defensive picture her mother had presented.

Because she was worried and frightened for her daughter, her mother had needed to minimize the impact that the separation had on Mary and to focus on her daughter's strengths and successes rather than her vulnerabilities. Mary herself had sought to avoid her own distress, and the extra worry that would cause her parents, by devoting herself to school work and to other achievements. It seemed that the much less important loss of her friend had revived her distress in the context of new school worries. These worries were also now given an extra meaning. It turned out that Mary had always harbored the fantasy that if she did really well she would bring her parents back together. The fear of failure threatened her with having to face the fact that this could never happen.

Brothers and sisters

In households where there has been a loss or separation, even ordinary problems may become especially highly charged. But in most families, general strife will often accompany early adolescence and outbursts often occur over issues which have hitherto been reasonably smoothly negotiated. The flash point between brothers and sisters is frequently over matters of, for example, differential allowances, or bed times, or the "You must be back by . . ." sort of issue.

In these contexts there is often felt to be a world of difference between a ten or eleven year-old's relationship with younger siblings and the twelve to fourteen year-old's. At twelve sensitivity to rights and prerogatives suddenly changes. Relationships with younger brothers and sisters may have muddled along, with not much attention being paid to the value of money, or effort expended on bothering to calculate the exact percentage more allowance that Johnny should have by virtue of being three years four months older than Susan.

At twelve, however, parents may encounter situations in which, for instance, the dishwashing may be done not only, as in Jake's family, begrudingly, or perhaps with a small bribe as before, but with the young teenager now putting a price on each plate, saucepan and item of cutlery. Jake would do elaborate, though pointless, calculations as to how to outdo his younger brother, who didn't care so much, or older sisters, who were by now more generous.

The major contests tend to occur with younger brothers and sisters rather than older ones. The twelve to fourteen year-olds become suddenly sensitive to differences of status and privilege which their superior years are felt to confer. They also begin to feel able to participate in the world of older brothers and sisters and not be the baby anymore. Lawrence described this in relation to his older brothers. "When I reached fourteen, if anyone picked on me they were there to support me. Tom would take me places—out to work with him. His friends would say, 'What are you bringing him along for?' Tom would say, 'If he's not coming, I'm not coming.' It was great."

By contrast, the more equal, albeit quarrelsome, relationships with younger brothers and sisters tend to change and a new kind of tension gets introduced into the more familiar types of conflict. What had been mildly teasing behavior is experienced as severely provocative. The threshold of tolerance becomes much lower and the tendency to hit back or even hit out is much greater. Parents are often driven to despair by this new edge to the hitherto manageable competitiveness and arguing. Bearing it as "just a phase," which is what it usually is, feels too much at times. It does not seem to trouble the young people themselves, who often feel more comfortable with the increasingly flexed muscles or barbed tongues than the adult world appreciates.

It is not unusual for twelve to fourteen year-olds to find themselves unexpectedly faced with a new baby in the family—a last child for parents who respond to the pain of their child becoming adolescent with a new pregnancy. Older teenagers may welcome this event as mobilizing the beginning of their own parenting feelings and impulses. A younger adolescent on the other hand, up until now the baby of the family, may be deeply angered by having to give up that special position and may respond with acute jealousy, often taking extreme forms of withdrawal, premature escape into alternative "worlds" or, more dramatically though not uncommonly with girls in particular, with their own pregnancy.

On the other hand, the appearance of a younger brother or sister may relieve a situation familiar to many, in which the young adolescent has found being smallest very hard and has cast him or herself in the role of black sheep of the family. Anne described herself as coming to some stark conclusions when she was twelve. "It was a nightmare. My older brother and sister seemed to be fine but I hated everything. I was so ugly and useless. I used to read the problem pages in magazines to find someone weirder than me. At home I just shut up—became completely silent for about two years. I just had a blank mask. My mom would say, 'What's wrong?' 'Nothing,' I would say. Or, 'What are you thinking?,' she would say. 'I don't know.' I felt being the youngest was so limiting. But also, I suppose it made things safe. Maybe it was my family keeping together and their expectations that kept me going. Lots of my friends didn't really come through."

The "rough justice" approach is often swept aside at this stage and demands for preferential treatment become more strident. Parents find themselves with major diplomatic problems on their hands, both wishing to confirm the adult strivings of their child, as being distinct now from the needs of younger brothers and sisters, and also keeping in mind the more infantile collapses and dependencies which frequently occur. Lawrence, now twenty, spoke warmly of his parents' capacity to offer him "a certain amount of rope to experiment with," but in a context in which "I knew there was a firm point at which the line would be drawn."

The eldest of Lawrence's three older brothers, Tom, had a less fortunate experience: "I think adolescence hit Tom very hard and unexpectedly. Adolescence was new to him but it was also new to my parents. They were quite an isolated couple, living just outside our small town, and didn't have much sense of what went on. Being treated differently from all your friends is an acute embarrassment and breeds deceit and trouble—at least it did with Tom. I think Tom suffered terribly because the rules in our family at that time were so different from other families. Dad's idea of being a father was to work all the time and bring in the money. He missed out on my older brothers. With Tom, Dad's idea of sorting it out was to give him a thick ear, but that changed a bit as we younger ones came along. That way of dealing with problems went out the window. I think he learned from his experience with Tom."

Sharing with other parents

Lawrence's account touches on many important issues, particularly, perhaps, the difficulty of reacting to the stress of this new experience of boundary-testing with measures which are neither too punitive nor too restrictive, nor too frighteningly permissive. In this context a sense of relationship with the "rules" of other families of young adolescents may be of great importance. Although the chance to talk to other parents at the "school gate" is now passed, at this next problematic stage a sense of connection on the parents' part with what is happening generally in the young adolescents' world may be of enormous value. Establishing acquaintances, or even friendship, with parents of similar aged children may take the heat off.

If there are some loosely agreed ideas among parents about reasonable bedtimes, how late they sleep in during the day, pocket money or allowances, parties and drinking and so on, it can be a great deal easier for parents to feel that a shared boundary is being established. For the young adolescent too, there may be a sense of relief that there is a limit-setting going on which is commonly agreed among a group of parents, rather than being an individual cross to bear—and therefore a source of particular grievance. A characteristic "skill' at this stage on the part of the twelve to fourteen year-old is the ability to split and divide the adult world against itself, particularly parent against parent, parent against teachers, or parent against other families. In a situation where the position is "I'm the *only* one who isn't allowed to stay over," head-on confrontation can often be avoided by means of a concerned, though not too intrusive, parental network of agreed limits, rather than each event being repeatedly fought out on individual battle grounds.

Conclusion

Twelve to fourteen year-olds, and possibly their parents too, are taking exciting steps forward at this time. Each child is finding his or her own unique way of negotiating the strange process of discovering who they are, and how different that may turn out to be from what they had always thought. Each step carries with it its own losses which are often difficult to adjust to, but also its own gains, which may not be as apparent at this time as later on.

The results can be both enriching and alarming. The weathering of these turbulent years, through understanding, tolerance, and honest response, may often expand and deepen relationships between parents and children, enabling each to separate, grow and change, and to establish the basis for lasting friendship and mutual respect.

FURTHER READING

What's Happening to My Body?- Boys, Lynda Madaras, Penguin 1989

What's Happening to My Body?- Girls, Lynda Madaras, Penguin 1989

Young People under Stress: A Parent's Guide, Sally Burningham, Virago, 1994

What's Happening to Me?, Peter Mayle, Pan 1993

It's OK To Be You. Feeling Good About Growing Up, Clare Patterson and Lyndsay Quilter, Piccolo 1991

THE AUTHOR

Margot Waddell originally trained as a child and adolescent psychotherapist, and has been on the staff of the Adolescent Department at the Tavistock Clinic since 1985. Before then, she worked for many years with adolescents and their problems in a College of Further Education. She has taught and written extensively about the adolescent world in a variety of contexts—child psychotherapy, training teachers, social workers and parents. She has experienced the adolescence of six of her own children and stepchildren.

UNDERSTANDING YOUR CHILD
TITLES IN THIS SERIES

Price per volume: $8.95 + $2.00 for shipping and handling

Please send your name, address and total amount to:

WARWICK PUBLISHING INC.
388 KING STREET WEST • SUITE 111
TORONTO, ONTARIO M5V 1K2